MW00721067

Granddaddy's Granddaughter

My Life in the Church

By Dawn Miller

Mill Lake Books

Copyright © 2022 by Dawn Miller
No part of this book may be reproduced in any form without written permission, except for brief quotations in critical reviews.

Mill Lake Books
Chilliwack, BC, Canada
https://jamescoggins.wordpress.com/mill-lake-books/

Cover design by Dean Tjepkema

Cover illustration: A painting of the original Port Coquitlam United Church by Alyce Shearer. Used by permission.

ISBN: 978-1-7771926-6-2

Table of Contents

Granddaddy Moses   Dad, Wesley

Dawn, age 5

Prologue

As I look back and review my life, I feel very blessed. Although I have experienced both good and bad circumstances, God enabled me to survive and grow within each experience. I feel grateful and satisfied.

Also as I look back, I recognize the central role that Christian churches have played in my life. My Granddaddy Moses Nixon emigrated from Ireland and became a Methodist circuit preacher in Manitoba. He rode on horseback to several small churches every week. My Dad, Wesley, did not agree with his evangelical father on many theological matters, yet in time he became a clergyman in the United Church. My younger years were closely intertwined with that church. I had the privilege of being a "preacher's kid." Granddaddy Moses baptized me when I was three years old, after my father had returned from World War II. I don't remember that day, but I have a few pictures of it. My granddaddy died soon after. Perhaps he said a special prayer of blessing over me. I know I was reading the Bible and asking questions at an unusually young age. Eventually I would leave my father's church and became involved in more evangelical churches. However, I am thankful for all the churches that were part of my life. They have been a positive influence.

Chapter 1
Early Childhood Memories
Cumberland and Port Alberni, B.C., 1948–1952

The United Church in Cumberland, on Vancouver Island, was the first church my dad went to as a minister after returning from World War II. I have very little memory of that church and only fleeting memories of the manse. Dad replaced his uncle, who was dying of cancer. The uncle's daughter was a war widow with a small daughter about my age. She moved to Cumberland to help her father and also my parents. While my parents were busy with their duties at the church in Cumberland and the subsidiary church in Campbell River, she looked after me. I attended kindergarten there.

Apparently, I didn't want to have anything to do with my father when he returned home from the war. I had been born just after he had left for overseas. He returned when I was three, so there was no understanding of the concept of a "father." I only knew that he took much of my mother's attention away from me, and I greatly resented his existence. This caused untold tensions between my parents. Also, his experiences on the battlefield changed my father in ways that would never be undone. It impacted his parenting and his marriage. Perhaps that is why I remained an only child.

Cumberland United Church

We moved to Port Alberni, also on Vancouver Island, in 1950, the summer before I was to start grade one. My father had been appointed minister of the United Church there. Tensions within the family were

4

somewhat less strained. My aunt was no longer there to care for me. Since my parents couldn't often afford a babysitter, I was often alone after school. Fortunately, the manse was right next to the church building. That church became my frequent alternate place to go seeking company. It became a core part of my existence. My time within that church would affect the rest of my life.

Nobody ever told me to go home. By nature, I was curious, friendly, and not at all shy. I was a cute child, with neat pigtails. There always seemed to be something going on at the church, and mostly people didn't seem to mind my presence. A few times, I was kindly escorted out of meetings, but then I could usually find someone else doing something in the building, and I would become involved there. I felt loved and needed.

I helped the janitors as they vacuumed and cleaned. They taught me some easy jobs and were great company. They seemed to appreciate my help. When something was being fixed or set up, I would lend a willing hand, serving as an errand girl. I was often sent to look for things or return things to their rightful place. I knew where everything was in that church.

When the organist practiced, I loved to listen. I remember playing with a doll on the floor or a pew nearby. Those old hymns penetrated my heart and soul as they became more and more familiar. Many seniors wish churches today would sing more of the old hymns and fewer of the modern tunes. People now want guitars and drums to make the music livelier. I am a senior, and my heart longs for those old hymns in the deepest way. I learned them before I learned any Bible stories.

Port Alberni United Church and manse

Sometimes, when the choir practiced, I would sit in the front pew and listen. Often the choir members would allow me to sit with them and pretend to be in the choir. The ladies would give me a hymn book and turn to the right pages. When they stood, I stood on the pew. They didn't let me practice the next Sunday's anthem with them. At those times, they would ask me to sit where the congregation would be and then ask my opinion on how it had sounded. They made me feel that my childish impressions mattered, even when I occasionally said something was wrong. Then they

6

smiled or laughed, and sometimes they even did the song over.

My love for church music started there. I wanted to be a church organist when I grew up. Some of my school chums started taking piano lessons. Many of them practiced after school, and they had to finish before they were allowed to go out to play. I wanted to do this too, so I asked my parents. I knew we didn't have a piano, but, being so close to the church, I thought I could practice there. However, the answer was "No." I couldn't believe it! I asked again in a few days. When I was turned down again, I asked why they wouldn't want me to learn. I suggested that perhaps when I was older I could play for Dad if the organist became sick. They said they didn't think I would practice but would waste their money. I begged to be allowed to try. If I neglected my lessons, then they could make me quit. The answer was still "No." That was the end of the subject for several years.

My greatest influence was from a lady who led the Explorer group. This was a group for girls in grades four to six, who met one day a week in the church basement after school. They learned songs, played games, did crafts, and heard Bible stories. I was too young to be a member. However, that leader really needed me. I met her at the church before the girls arrived, and she got me to do the craft for the day to see how it would work for a child. I enjoyed crafts, so this was fun. Then she let me set out all the supplies for each girl and help those having difficulty. She let me clean up all the mess afterward and put things away.

Before the craft, she let me give out supplies for games and put them away. If one team was short a member, I filled in. I got to help her hold up pictures as she told Bible stories. There I learned so much about the Bible and God. In fact, I remember more from Explorers than from the Sunday school classes I must have attended. When it was all over and everything was cleaned up, she asked me to walk her home and carry her supply bag. She always rewarded me with a hug and sometimes a candy once we reached her home. I loved feeling useful and needed.

I do not remember ever being reprimanded by my folks, so somehow I must have managed to be home when expected. I received many gifts from church people. I remember the beautiful dolls, some small, some larger. They took up an important part of my room and gave me someone to talk, sing, and read to, and someone to hug. I was therefore never really alone.

Time with My Parents

I don't have clear recollections of my parents' activities at the time. I was too busy with school, my various church activities, and dolls.

During the time we lived there, my father oversaw the building of an addition to the front of the church, giving more space for the growing congregation.

Dad also started very affordable church camps at Parksville. We had always camped there in the summer, so maybe he made an agreement with the owner. Somehow he procured some giant army tents. That camp was right by the beach and is still there, although it is now very modern. This may have been before church camps became common. Many children slept in one tent, and another was used for the cooks, the nurse, storage, etc.

One summer, my mother decided that since Dad was involved in camps, she and I would travel by train to visit her parents on a Saskatchewan farm. It was important to her that I be a perfect child there. Apparently, I did not measure up, no matter how hard I tried. I caused chaos by disappearing often. I had to hide in bins under straw because that big, honking goose kept chasing me. I thought extra strawberries could be stored in my pockets. I disliked the outdoor toilet. Eventually, I became ill and listless, and the doctor said I might be homesick.

We returned home early. Mom thought I missed Dad, so she took me to the camp. He was suspiciously pleased that I wanted to see him, but he was too busy directing the camp to spend much time with me. I remember sleeping at the end of the huge tent. During the day, I was left in the care of the cooks. Again, I was able to help and visit with them. When they didn't have time for me, I was free to do as I wished. The only rule I was given was to not swim unless with an adult from the camp. I loved gathering pretty pink shells at the beach and wading through the warm puddles when the tide was out. I still love Parksville, and it remains my favorite place to camp.

Looking back, I am sure that I would have been just as happy returning to Port Alberni and being with Mom. Adjusting to Saskatchewan had been strange for me. Also, I had caught the tension in my mother when I didn't act just right. Over the years, I usually spent more time with Dad than Mom. However, I greatly valued the times she and I spent together with no one else present. She did many special things for and with me.

I remember breaking my right arm and at the same time developing chicken pox. The itching under the cast was terrible. I had to stay home from school. A friend brought me work from school, so I could keep up. My mother spent time teaching me to print with my left hand. I remember that when I returned to the school, there was a substitute teacher. Our regular teacher had maintained very poor discipline and had lost control of that class. Perhaps that was why the substitute was quite mean. In those days, being lefthanded was discouraged. However, the use of my left hand was a temporary but necessary measure. Maybe that teacher did not see the cast as she cracked her pointer hard over my knuckles while I was proudly showing off my ability to print. I refused to do any further work that day. I told my parents I would not return to school until

10

she was gone. That is my only negative memory of Port Alberni up until that point.

Some Upsetting Changes

That fall, however, some surprising and upsetting changes came to my small, happy, secure world. Something seemed wrong, at least at home. Mostly I escaped to the church or to my dolls, so I didn't really hear much of what was happening.

One evening, my mother took me, my dolls, and a blanket out to the manse steps. I was forbidden to go to the church or go back into the house until she came for me. As I played with my dolls, I looked up and down the street. There were so many cars, more than usual for a church service, wedding, or funeral. The door to the house was open. Through the screen, I could see Mom talking on the phone, and she was crying. I have no memory of how that evening ended.

It seemed like the next day that we were moving, immediately! Furniture was being put into storage, and we were to go to Vancouver and live in a motel. A big suitcase was put on my bed, and I was told to start packing. All of my dolls with their clothes and furniture would not fit into the suitcase. I decided the dolls needed to stay together, so I took the extra clothes to my parents to pack. When they saw I had not packed anything except my dolls, I was told I could take only ONE doll and my old panda bear.

In later years, I became an integral part of church leadership. I now understand that whatever had transpired within the church was serious. Perhaps my father had done something wrong, or perhaps he was the victim of malicious gossip. This had to have caused great turmoil in my parents' relationship and fear for their future. Therefore, it is to their credit that when their little daughter dissolved into a weeping puddle, they decided something had to be done about the doll situation.

Following many phone calls, Mom arranged that other girls in the community would "adopt" my dolls. Mom and Dad helped me gather them together in the back seat of the car, each with their own luggage. That evening, Dad drove me from house to house, and I was sent to each door with a doll. I'd ring the doorbell, and a girl and mother would emerge and show excitement and gratitude about adopting my doll. Between stops, Dad talked to me and explained that I really had too many dolls to adequately care for and other girls had fewer than I had. He said I was being very unselfish and was helping both my dolls and these other girls. When we finally got home, Mom gave me a hug and told me I was a brave, kind little girl and she was very proud of me. She fussed over me until I was sleeping. A very positive spin was put on adoption. Much later, my husband and I would foster a handicapped girl for sixteen years and adopt four boys.

We departed for Vancouver quickly after that. I attended three schools that year and lived in four homes. Life changed for us all. During the next two and a half years, my parents both worked in jobs not connected with the church. Dad later explained in his memoir that he took this time to fully emotionally recover from his war experiences. I know that was truly necessary. Following that break, he would return to a successful ministry in many churches in British Columbia and Saskatchewan, serving until he retired.

I will always be thankful to that church in Port Alberni. Everyone there treated me as a valuable, lovable little person. They built me up. Those people were all that really mattered in my small world. I didn't feel shy around people as I had not experienced rejection, yet.

I didn't continue much of a relationship with my one remaining doll. She seemed sad as if she was missing her sisters. My panda bear was loved with greater intensity until he fell apart and somehow disappeared. Another panda appeared, but he didn't know me, so he remained an ornament. I wondered if the janitors and organist and choir people in Port Alberni missed me. I knew I greatly missed them! I knew the Explorer leader would have difficulty managing without my invaluable help. I didn't know it then, but about nine years later she and I would joyfully meet again, when we were both leaders at Moorecroft church camp.

Meanwhile, I now had to deal with the real world without my previous support connections. Life was never going to be as easy again. However, the church at Port Alberni made me a stronger and better person, and I am very grateful. I learned there that the church can be an invaluable and essential foundation to any child's life. It can enable all people, including children, to feel sheltered, loved, and needed. This relationship, in time, can foster a fuller understanding of God and a personal faith in Jesus Christ.

Subsequent churches where my dad would be minister did not have the manse next door. There were some privacy advantages with that separation. On the other hand, most children will not have the opportunity to live next to their church or feel free to run within it as I had been privileged to do for a few formative years.

What can be done for our children to fill that place that Port Alberni provided me? Much emphasis has been put into Sunday school curricula and children's features. Often a lot of money is spent on materials to entertain children. However, children need more than entertainment and teaching. They need to feel loved. They need to feel useful and important. We must include children in the everyday work and mundane operation of the church. Programs and worship times are only a small portion of what the church family can offer children when they are young. Early involvement in church can provide a foundation of self-worth.

Spiritual understanding, faith, and commitment can be built on this foundation. This strength can last a lifetime.

The Port Alberni church gave me that foundation. Future life storms would rock my life. However, Port Alberni helped me build inner strength and purpose so I would never completely disintegrate in times of strife.

Chapter 2
A Very Different Life
Vancouver and Ladysmith, B.C., 1953–1955

My first report card for grade three was from Port Alberni. The second was from a school in Vancouver. The third and fourth report cards of that year, plus all of the next year's, were from Ladysmith.

Following our hasty departure from Port Alberni, we moved to Vancouver for a short time. My parents first moved into a motel for a brief time until they found a house to rent temporarily. Even in the house, however, we did not have all of our belongings. We used our camping gear and slept in our sleeping bags on air mattresses. We even had a small camping table and folding chairs.

Dad took me to my new school in Vancouver and got me registered the first day, and I settled into my new classroom, at least somewhat. This building was a big, imposing, older structure. There were several classes for each grade. My parents had told me to not tell anyone where we were from, where we lived, or what my father's job had been. The loss of my dolls was my first childhood trauma. Not knowing where I lived became the reason for the second.

When Dad drove me to school the second day, there were no children in the playground. Dad thought we must be late, so he gave me a note before driving off. However, when I entered the school, I found nobody there at all! I sat on the hallway floor and sobbed in fear. An unfortunate janitor found me. He explained that the teachers had a conference meeting in another school. Not knowing where we lived became a huge problem for him and for my teacher, whom he called at the conference. If I had been free to tell them we were living in a motel, that would have been helpful to them. Soon Dad heard on the radio about the conference and came looking for me. I remember sobbing as we drove home. I was so familiar with Port Alberni. Had a problem developed there, I would have run home or into the church seeking help. I was seriously displaced in Vancouver.

Also, it was in Vancouver that I first experienced bullying. I wore orthopedic boots and spoke with a slight speech impediment. My former classmates had grown up with me and were used to these. In Vancouver, my quirks were the focus of taunting. Also, my not knowing where we came from or where we lived seemed strange to my classmates. I was jeeringly called, "Don't Know." Bullying would continue to be part of my life. I was fortunate that the dear people in the church at Port Alberni had instilled within me the knowledge that I was a special, important, and precious child. I understood that these new people just didn't understand this yet. My underlying sense of self-worth enabled me to become a survivor.

The Alley Group

Very soon, we moved to Ladysmith, back on Vancouver Island. We lived in an apartment above the bakery on the main street. My parents both got jobs at MacMillan Bloedel in Chemainus. Dad worked in the lumber yard, and Mom was a secretary in the office. We got our furniture back, and we started the next short chapter of our lives. Unfortunately, bullying continued at my new school. Perhaps I had gradually lost some of my self-confidence and had developed a persona that invited mean responses and teasing.

However, I was a part of the "alley group." Each of the stores of the main street had an apartment above it which the owners lived in or rented out—like ours over the bakery. The children of these dwellings seemed to hang together regardless of gender or age. The back alley was a safe place for us at that time, and we seemed to all get along. This was really my first experience of play involving other children. Formerly, I had been fully occupied with church activities and my dolls.

Most of us had one feature in our small yard that provided an opportunity for some activity. Ours had a large, flat cement pad so that we girls had continuous hopscotch tournaments. My parents had to be careful not to move each girl's chains and thus disturb the markings for when we started the next day.

One boy's father fixed us an old lady's bike. His son was in charge, but we were to take turns. I learned to ride a bike there. We were told to never leave the alley, as the other streets were so steep.

My parents were away working when I left for school and returned each day, so I was truly a "latchkey kid." However, they planned a few treats for me. Every day when I heard the pans banging, I was allowed to go down to the bakery and pick one loaf of bread or a dozen baked goods to surprise my parents.

Also, my mother took me to the public library and got me my own card. Young children were not usually allowed to sign out books unless accompanied by a parent. However, Mom explained the situation, and an exception was made. I loved going to the library and loitering there. Soon, the librarian let me help stamp books and even return some to the shelves.

Church Questions

There had been no church contact when we were in Vancouver. However, in Ladysmith, we became part of the United Church again. The three of us were welcomed, and friends were made. Both of my parents became Sunday school teachers, Mom was in the choir, and Dad often filled in for the minister when needed.

Mom and I attended Brownies. She was a leader. I earned different badges to put on my little brown uniform. Mom and I used to practice tying knots and doing various types of bandages together—so I could earn pins and she could prepare to teach.

The three of us went on a designated school bus many Saturdays to ice skate in the rink at Nanaimo. My parents spent quite a bit of time teaching me. Other than camping, this was my first memory of doing things with my parents—and it was good.

Somehow, I acquired a small black children's Bible with a zipper all around it pulled by a cross. It had pictures, and it was a complete Bible. I started reading the Gospel of Matthew. Since I was just learning to read, this was hard work, but I kept at it every night, and I started to pray. I wish I knew who gave me that precious Bible—or where it went. However, the important thing is that I had it for many years and it gave me a start in reading the Scriptures daily.

A few things began to go wrong between myself and the church. I seemed out of place at Sunday school. I have no clear bad memories, so I don't know what was wrong. However, I remember being moved from one class to another. It could not have been a behavior issue. My parents were teachers, and they would have heard about it and straightened that out. Nothing was said or explained. I began to feel not wanted and begged my parents to allow me to skip Sunday school. I said I would walk over later and join them for church.

21

They rejected this idea. One Sunday, a teacher from an older class kindly asked me if I'd like to come and help her. I don't remember assisting her much, but I know I stayed with that class. It is surprising that only a few of my peers initially asked "Why…?" before being cut off.

Knowing me in subsequent situations, I expect I was likely asking too many questions in the previous classes. I was already taking God, the Bible, and faith seriously at a young age. Perhaps I was afraid to question the last teacher, or perhaps she explained things better. Maybe I feared the older students and kept quiet. However, I felt content and secure once again.

Once when my father was preaching, he told the story of Jesus walking on water. When Peter tried to walk towards Him, he looked down at the waves and sank. I had just read that passage at home and understood it to mean what it said. However, Dad explained that this was symbolic, written to encourage us not to look down at life's problems but rather to look up and trust in God. Later, I asked Dad why Jesus couldn't have walked on water since He created it. Dad said I'd understand more when I was older. I was only eight!

Following an infant baptism, again I questioned my father. Jesus was dedicated by his parents at the temple when He was a baby. However, He wasn't baptized until He was an adult. Why were babies being baptized in church? Again, I was told I'd understand as I grew older.

Later, I came to see that these questions were the beginnings of my eventual breaking away from my father's liberal theology. I was leaning towards the evangelistic faith of my granddaddy, Moses Nixon. It is true that we don't "inherit" faith as we might hair or eye color. I never spent much time with Granddaddy, as I only saw him a few times before he died. I had never talked with or met anyone who understood the Bible differently from Dad. Later, an aunt remarked that I talked just like Grandpa. Interesting indeed! History came full circle.

This Ladysmith part of my story shows that church involvement must be central to the life of a family, not merely a small part of it. Here, I wasn't the minister's daughter. No longer did I have that unique reason to feel that church was important to me. Here, I was not free to run around in the church as I had been accustomed to doing. However, my parents continued to make church a central part of our lives. It seemed it did not matter why we had left the previous church. My parents and I were accepted and respected. Church support for us enabled a worthwhile spiritual, emotional, and social life to continue in spite of previous problems. Regardless of what caused my unhappiness in Sunday school, an unusual solution had been found that suited me. Our small family felt settled and relaxed as a result. I know my dad found healing and strength during that time. Following this brief interval, he returned to the ministry and remained in it, even past retirement age.

Often, some children come into Sunday school or church activities and present various problems to the leaders. I am convinced that churches must genuinely seek to adjust their programs to suit the needs of each child and family. It seems that this has not been done often enough in churches in the past few decades. Could that be part of the reason Sunday school and other Christian education endeavors have declined? Society is suffering as a result. It's not too late to reverse the trend. Maybe we can learn from our past. The main thing that churches need is not fancy media, but individual love and concern. More attention and effort must be focused on younger people, as they are the future of church life for the generations ahead.

Chapter 3
More Formative Experiences
Port Coquitlam, B.C., 1955–1960

We moved to Port Coquitlam in 1955, the summer before I would start grade five. I would be part of this and one more church move with my parents. Grandpa Moses, under the Methodist Church, had been required to move at least every four years. This was somewhat the pattern my father followed, although he extended this to five or six years. He grew up believing that church moves were healthy for both the minister and the church. A change brings forth different workers and new ways of doing things. My dad felt it was better to leave a church when the congregation was sad to lose him, rather than waiting until people were wishing for a change.

Five or six years seemed like a lifetime for me after the turbulent past two years. Dad had promised to buy me a bike if we moved to a flatter town than Ladysmith. I noticed that many of the streets of Port Coquitlam were quite flat. The next day, before unpacking continued, we went to buy a beautiful, three-speed girl's bike. I was very excited and happy.

The summer was somewhat boring as I didn't know many other children. However, we went camping and got used to the new church. Dad carried out some renovations in the manse after getting approval from the church. It was a huge, very old, beautiful house, much too big for the three of us. The heat came from a wood furnace in the basement that Dad had to stoke. He certainly did not want the work and expense of heating the whole house and rearranged rooms so we could all live on the main floor. However, in the near future, I would be allowed to have sleepovers with my friends, and we had three bedrooms and a bathroom upstairs to ourselves. For those occasions, Dad opened up some heat vents for us. We would be the last minister's family to live in that home.

Church manses were an important aspect of my life. Until more recently, most churches owned a manse as a home for the minister. The minister was given a housing allowance for its maintenance. Every year, the elders or the leaders of the ladies' group would come to see if anything needed to be fixed. Ministers' families usually felt this was an "inspection" of sorts, which involved prior cleaning and straightening things up! In time, ministers would prefer to choose their own home. Churches then sold or rented the manses. However, my parents always made the best of whatever manse the church provided. Never did I hear them wish for anything different or better. When they retired, they bought an older home and worked hard to adapt it to suit themselves. I think that the variety of manses we lived in, plus my parents' acceptance of them, prepared me well for the years ahead. This would play a part in my future willingness to live in whatever home my husband could provide. I never felt I wanted a better home or expensive, unnecessary renovations.

Port Coquitlam United Church 1925-1965

Mom and Dad did make some changes in the manses, but they were fairly minor and cosmetic. They made more changes in the Port Coquitlam house than in any they lived in after that. For example, Dad's wish for us all to live on one floor necessitated him making a small bathroom off the kitchen.

There were two large pillars in the entranceway between the living room and the dining room. My parents used the dining room as a combination living room and dining room, making the former living room into their bedroom. My bedroom was the den off the main room. It even had a fireplace! However, those pillars made it difficult to install any kind of door to my parents' bedroom. They had numerous discussions about whether the pillars were decorative or supportive. Could or should they be removed? Should they ask permission to remove them? No agreement was reached.

One night, my mother went out for the evening. Dad assembled his saw and other tools by the pillars. He said he was going to remove the pillars, no matter what Mom said. I remember great excitement as I watched him saw those pillars away. Would the ceiling fall down? He must have been sure he knew what he was doing because he didn't ask me to evacuate just in case. However, he did make sure I was sleeping before Mom returned.

The church was a few miles from the manse, so I could not spend as much time in it as I had done in those formative years in Port Alberni. However, the people were very nice to us. Many came to help with renovations, and others invited us for supper. Somehow, I felt more settled. My parents seemed to be much happier being back to their original way of living.

Relationships

It was exciting when school started and I was able to meet more children my age. I met Ingrid, and we became bosom pals. It was hard to believe she had lived so close to me all summer and we hadn't seen each other. She and her family had emigrated from Germany the year before. She had four siblings, two brothers and two sisters. She was second oldest. The children all spoke English well, but the parents didn't. Therefore, only German was spoken in the home. It would soon become apparent that the most significant aspect of this family for my own life was that they were Baptists.

Even before I met Ingrid, as I read the Bible more, I had come to believe what it said in a very literal way. When I talked with Ingrid's family, I was excited to learn that their beliefs seemed very similar to mine. I was very happy to learn that there were other people who believed as I did. It wasn't a matter of me not being old enough to understand fully. When I was in their church, I saw a baptistery at the front. I didn't know what it was. When I asked, they explained their beliefs about adult baptism. Here also, they believed as I did! I told my father this. He said that the family were nice people but they were quite uneducated and so were incapable of understanding the truth except in a childlike, literal way. So now, in his view, education was the foundation of faith, not age.

This family sometimes invited me for supper, which was followed by family devotions. Usually, they did these in German. However, when I was there, they asked the oldest boy to lead in English. Finally, I told them I would prefer if they did their devotions in German. Somehow, it felt better when they read the Bible and prayed in their own language. Even though I could not understand the words, I understood the feeling, and it was comforting.

Ingrid and I shared many adventures, and if this was a memoir, I'd fill pages with accounts of what we did. Again, I often came home to an empty house. However, I had a bike, and Ingrid was only a block away. I had met other friends as well.

Meanwhile, in our church life, I started to see how important interpersonal connections were within a congregation. My father always expressed genuine interest in all the people of his congregation. He never wanted a big city church; he preferred a church where he could know all the people. He'd offer support, encouragement, and practical help when he saw people struggling. My parents were active in community affairs and showed interest and care for everyone. That was a life lesson for me. All people, especially within a church, should seek to show God's love through meaningful concern for others. Often, seemingly trivial interactions make a big difference in how people feel about the church and ultimately in how they respond to God.

I'd later learn that not all ministers were as willing or as gifted as Dad, to be able to involve themselves with other people's struggles. His passion for people made me see that it was important for everyone within a congregation to carefully watch for people who are suffering hurt, confusion, or pain. Every member of the church should be willing to get involved in helping in some way. This includes helping people within the church but also helping people in the general community. There are many ways to help. Even introverted people can lay a kind hand on a shoulder or say a few words of encouragement. Practical help can uplift and assist. Many people have been hurt in various ways by church people. However, within that same church, others can offer compassion and healing.

The Port Coquitlam United Church continued to provide me and my family with the essential foundational security needed for a worthwhile life. Our life revolved around the activities of the church. It was a very busy church. Mom was in the choir and belonged to a few ladies' groups. There were frequent dinners in the church basement. The Sunday school was large. It was difficult to try to fit all the classes into separate rooms after the general opening. So, Dad worked on renovations in the church, often commenting that he had to "subdivide the broom closets." When we moved from there, the church would start a building project for a new church.

White Gift Sunday

I have a wealth of memories from that church. One was White Gift Sunday, which was just before Christmas. A tree was erected on the front stage. On that day, the Sunday school children came up in classes and placed gifts wrapped in plain white paper under the tree. On one corner was written what age or gender the gift would suit. These would be included in large hampers for needy families in the community. We were each encouraged to bring a children's gift. It was to be either new or "as good as new." Children were encouraged to give sacrificially. When the adults came, they placed food items in a large white box at the church entrance.

This was one time when, as Dad's daughter, I benefited more than the average child. He let me help him assemble all the contributions into boxes for families. Each box had a label attached which included the names and ages of the children. My job was to distribute the gifts as fairly as possible. I put a Christmas stamp over any writing and attached a tag with a child's name. Sometimes there were even gifts for adults. Dad distributed the canned goods among the boxes. Later, a turkey or a ham, plus some fresh produce, was added. In later years, other groups in the church did this job, but for a few years I had the privilege of sharing this significant experience with him.

I went with Dad when he delivered these hampers. It took a few days. Some families greeted the hampers with great relief and thankfulness. If we were invited in, I was to talk to the children and put the gifts under the tree, giving Dad an opportunity to talk to the adults. However, at some of the homes, we were not greeted as excitedly. Some of the places were very messy, and it was hard to find a place to put the hamper. Some recipients expressed little gratitude, and in some homes the children were allowed to tear the paper off their gifts instead of saving them for Christmas.

As we drove away, I asked Dad if these families would get a hamper the next year. This gave him an opportunity to explain to me how poverty can change the attitudes of people. However, this did not mean their need did not exist. Our job was to provide help but leave how it was accepted and used to them.

In later years, White Gift Sunday became more efficient. Instead of gifts from the Sunday school, families donated money in white envelops. This was used to buy items for each hamper. However, I feel the meaning was lost for the children. It was more significant for the children to each be asked to put an actual gift for a needy child under the tree.

Camp Life

Summer camps were also very important to the life of the church. Church funds supplemented entry fees for children who could not otherwise afford to go. The first camp I went to was at Cultus Lake. In my last years there, a boat launch was being built right behind the camp. This eventually resulted in the demise of that camp. However, when we lived in Port Coquitlam, it was very active. Both of my parents went to be leaders, at different times, leaving me with the alternate parent. I also went to that camp several times. In those days, camps went for two weeks.

The children in each cabin were required to make a religious centerpiece inside the door of the cabin that would help center their minds on God. We could use whatever natural materials we found to create this and even change it often. I loved that, as well as the numerous camp activities. A leader slept in the cabin with us. I remember that, at one of the first camps, I became very attached to our cabin leader. She talked to me about God and Jesus and seemed very accepting of my understanding of the Bible. I remember being very upset when the camp ended, realizing that I would likely never see her again.

That leader encouraged me to take swimming lessons and take the tests. In those days, we could get Red Cross swimming lessons at those camps. At the end of the camp, someone would come to test us. If we passed the tests, we were given the appropriate certificates. I earned all the certificates, one each year, until I needed to take Life Saving. That class wasn't offered at the camp, so my mom drove me to classes in New Westminster for this. I passed, but, at age fifteen, I was too young, so I was given the Junior Life Guard badge. The next year, I could do the same test and get the Senior Life Guard certificate. The plan was that when I was old enough, I could get a paid job at a church camp in the summers as a lifeguard and swimming instructor. However, the second test didn't happen. I was with a group of friends at a river in town, even though my parents had asked me to not swim there but to use the safer swimming pool. My friend disappeared in the river and drowned. I felt shaken and guilty, as I had been right beside her and hadn't been aware she had been taken by the current. However, the church camp provided me good lessons. Even as a senior, I love swimming and am safe doing so.

I also went to Moorecroft Camp on Vancouver Island. It was a CGIT girls' camp. CGIT was Canadian Girls in Training, the version of Brownies and Explorers for older girls. I belonged to CGIT in Port Coquitlam, so I could attend this camp. My parents drove me to a church in Vancouver. A bus was there, and it took us on the ferry and then to the camp. That camp was more rugged than Cultus Lake. The bus could only get us to the cookhouse. Then, wheelbarrows were used to transport our luggage a significant distance to the cabins. Three times a day, we walked back to that cookhouse. I was the only one from our church going there, but I met many nice girls. The first year, I was in a cabin with a very devout girl who believed much as I did.

The camp was on a small inlet on the ocean. When the tide was out, it was empty. However, we were never allowed to walk on that sand as the tide came in very quickly. Apparently, some deaths had occurred earlier. Anyone breaking this rule was sent home immediately. We used to have "vespers" in the evening at the chapel right by the water. Many candles were used, and it was very inspiring. I felt very close to God there.

Later, I became a junior leader in that camp. In future years, it was sold and became a beautiful, rugged regional park. Many years later, my husband and I were camping nearby at Parksville. I took him to that camp and explained where everything used to be. The first time we went, one of the cabins remained, so he could see how it had once been. It happened to be the first cabin I had stayed in. That location is a wonderful place to go on a hike or just sit and feel God's majesty. The second time we were there, we were sitting on logs quite high up so we could watch the tide come rushing into the inlet. Our cell phone rang. It was our son from Toronto, and he had some very sad news. It was such a wonderful place to be while we had that painful discussion with him. Once again, we were very grateful for the natural evidence of God's presence.

Things Go Wrong

We had been in Port Coquitlam for five years before things started to go wrong for me. All was not well at home. Neither was life well for me. Ingrid developed into a beautiful teenager and became boy crazy. I felt ugly and undesirable. Other friends started drinking and smoking, and I was left out. I did well at school, so I focused on that, maybe to an unhealthy degree. Following the first set of midterm exams in grade nine, I didn't "feel well." I was unable to explain this feeling. That report card showed all high marks. However, my "heavy" feelings remained. My next set of exams indicated something was very wrong, as I was failing or barely passing most subjects. A meeting was called with my teachers, my parents, the principal (a man from our church), and myself. The school had assumed I had become too involved in social activities. My father said that sadly the opposite was true, as I rarely left my room. I tried to explain that although I did read my schoolbooks, I couldn't seem to remember anything. I didn't know what was wrong except that I "didn't feel well." Doctors were seen, nothing was found wrong, and everyone was confused. I was told to straighten out and rectify my "attitude" immediately. I felt tremendous guilt, as I didn't know how.

I later learned the illness was called depression. I had never heard that word then. If anyone had suspected it and mentioned it to my parents, an angry response would have been evoked. I needed help, which I didn't get. Things became so bad that I started to think of ways to kill myself and eventually came up with a plan. I had ample opportunity, as often I was left alone. Only one thing stopped me. I thought about how my funeral would be. It would be in our church.

Perhaps a minister friend of Dad's would do it, as by now he was active in the denomination and knew many of the other ministers. But how would the people in the church feel? They had been nothing but kind to me. How could I impose such agony upon my family and church friends? It was indeed fortunate that the church was so important to me.

On the other hand, it was unfortunate that I didn't get some counseling. I know now that it is important to deal with teenage depression. Otherwise, this pattern of depression could be wired into the brain as it completes its growth, resulting in future problems.

Although I was very young, I managed to reason my way through my confusing emotions to some degree. I knew I was missing my friend Ingrid. She was still there but was less interested in spending time with me. She made me feel inadequate. I wondered what I could do to somehow replace the fun times I had spent with her after school and on weekends. I remembered my earlier wish to take piano lessons. The church was further from home than the earlier church, but I could walk to it. In fact, when walking home from school, I walked past it.

Of course, my father again refused to support this idea. I wasn't even getting my schoolwork done, so why would he pay for more work for me to do? I seriously considered this. However, I thought that maybe if I had to spend time practicing, I'd be motivated to finish my schoolwork and still have time for music. Across the street was a big home that had been made into a seniors' facility. I lied about my age and got a job there washing dishes and carrying trays. I used some of this money for piano lessons.

I found a lady who taught music lessons and lived quite near the school. I went to see her and told her I wanted to learn to play church hymns. She told me that this would be too difficult and I would need to start with the basics. When she saw my disappointment, she said she would spend some time helping me with a hymn at the end of each lesson if I had done all she'd asked me to do well enough and there was still time. It seemed like a good compromise.

It did work, to a degree. Nowadays, when older children or adults want to start learning to play, there are appropriate books that will appeal to them. However, she had me doing childish pieces. Nevertheless, they taught me what I needed to learn, so I persevered. Most weeks, we had time for her to help me with a hymn. She always seemed surprised at how well I managed them.

This arrangement seemed to alleviate my feeling of emptiness somewhat, and things went quite well for many months. I practiced on the way home from school if the church was empty. Also, I walked there on Saturdays to spend a greater amount of time. This was all time I had earlier spent with Ingrid. I started to feel better about life. My schoolwork improved slightly.

Unfortunately, one day, my boss at the care home asked for evidence of my age. I had to admit I had lied, and he immediately fired me. He was foolish to have confronted me just as I was starting to do dishes. I responded by walking out, leaving him with all the dishes! However, I was sad to leave. I had come to love the residents I took trays to. Also, I had met some slightly older girls who had been friendly to me.

Nothing was said at home, but soon my parents realized I was no longer going to the care home to work. When they asked, I had to admit I had lied to get the job so I could have money for piano lessons. I had saved up some of this money and would be able to continue lessons for a while longer. However, I told my teacher I wouldn't be able to continue much longer and asked if she could please teach me only the most important skills. This would eliminate hymns.

To my surprise, my dad offered to continue paying for my lessons, and I could save my remaining money for other things I might like to buy for myself. He also purchased an old pump organ from a church and put it into my bedroom. No matter what had changed their mind about music, I was pleased that my parents finally were supportive of me.

A Perfect First Boyfriend

Soon life improved in a social way as well. Our teen Sunday school teacher started a midweek youth group. We were only allowed to come to the Wednesday social if we had attended Sunday school; only very rare exceptions were tolerated. At one point, the leader even hired a square dance instructor to give us all lessons. My mom made me some new skirts with stiff, wide waistbands. Together with new blouses, these suited me well, and I even wore them to school. I started to feel better about myself. We took turns bringing lunch to share after our dancing lessons, and our class expanded greatly. Through it, I met my first boyfriend.

One evening a boy asked if he could walk me home after the social. He had not been part of the church but had become interested in me at school. To impress me and my parents, he started attending many functions in our church. At first, the church people were somewhat taken by surprise, as he was from "the wrong part of town." His hair and clothes made him look like a "hood." However, he soon made a few changes and impressed most of them. God must have sent him to me. He was the perfect first boyfriend. He thought I was beautiful yet never acted inappropriately, even when we were alone. We laughed a lot together. I started to feel my "heaviness" lift.

Gradually, due to him, I started to develop a social group of kids, not all of whom were connected to the church. We even attended some socials together, mostly in the homes of his friends. This was my first introduction to social drinking. I had a few drinks, but that never became a problem for me. It made me feel part of the crowd and less "the preacher's kid."

However, our social life connections with the church continued, as well as our very long walks together. Every Saturday, we would meet at the church after my piano practice and go for chips at the café.

That year, my dad started a "communicant's class." This was preparation for membership or confirmation on Palm Sunday. Most of us were sixteen or seventeen. I was promised a new dress. My boyfriend was taking the class. All was well. However, following some religious discussion at home, my mother announced that I should not become a member of the United Church. My beliefs did not align with Dad's or the church's. What!? No new dress? What about my boyfriend? I retorted that I believed as much as most of the others in the class. The main difference between me and the others was that I asked Dad more questions, whereas they were much less interested. They didn't know or care enough to have any questions. Dad had to agree, and so I became a member of the United Church. I feel this was important to my development, even if in later years I would leave that church. I was given the "right hand of fellowship" and allowed to take my first communion. It meant that the church accepted me as a reasonable, responsible adult. This meant a lot, especially at that time.

My school marks started to improve but didn't reach the top status I had enjoyed in younger grades. Young love replaced depression and kept my mind from concentrating too much on my books. However, my parents were relieved that I came home with passing grades. The less than stellar marks at least were the result of a healthier teenage mind.

More Difficulties

I started to come out of the darkness. However, other problems continued, which Dad felt could possibly be resolved by a move. We had been in Port Coquitlam six years. He resigned, and that summer we were to move to Abbotsford, B.C. I would be going into grade eleven and very much wanted to graduate with my friends. I didn't want to lose my boyfriend. I was totally devastated! I appealed to my parents to not move. When that pleading failed, I suggested they seek room and board for me with some church family in Port Coquitlam. Every weekend, I would take the bus to Abbotsford and spend the weekend and holidays with them. Again, my parents adamantly refused. I became a very angry daughter. I hated my parents, the church…and maybe even God! I warned them I would not be part of their new church life.

The Port Coquitlam church had a huge farewell event for us. My parents were given a beautiful standing lamp. I was given a lovely ring. That ring was very important to me. It showed that the people in the church cared for me as well as my parents. Every effort had been made to get a ring that was in the popular style of that time yet suited my hand in spite of the chewed nails. It gave me a reason to take better care of my hands. However, it made me even more sad to leave.

I am very grateful to that church for nurturing me through those important formative years. I can remember many fun times with various church groups. Everyone was kind and encouraging. That church was essential in my life and made me stronger for the years ahead.

Chapter 4
Questions and Answers
Abbotsford, B.C., 1960–1966

The day we moved from Port Coquitlam, my boyfriend came as the moving truck was being loaded. When it left town, we all followed it in the family car. When we were closer to his home, we let him out. We had a teary farewell. From time to time, we would continue to see each other, and we would write frequent letters. However, as is typical of first loves, eventually we both moved on.

In a bold but quiet manner, I reminded my parents not to expect me to be as active in church life as I had been. I told them I would try to act in a manner that would not bring embarrassment to them, but beyond that I was simply living with them at their insistence. The climate within the car was quiet but not accusatory or threatening. When we reached the manse in Abbotsford, I was surprised to find that we had a beautiful, modern home. It was a floor and a half. There was one bedroom and a bathroom downstairs and two bedrooms and a full bathroom upstairs. I had a whole upper half floor to myself for a year. Later, my mother would take in female boarders to help finance my future education costs. Mom and I quickly lost any hostile or hurt thoughts as we excitedly put things away.

That summer, as usual after a move, was somewhat boring, as I met few friends. My parents and I went on a long, three-week camping trip. This would be my last year going with them in the summer. In the following summers, I would have jobs to help earn needed money. I can't remember even where we went that year, but it was a cooling down time for the three of us. Soon we were back home, and in August my parents started to prepare for church activities to resume in the fall. There had been controversy within the church the previous year regarding music, and Dad had a few obstacles to overcome starting out.

I had to prepare emotionally for entering a new school and a new set of activities. Soon I would be confronted with activities I "should" be in. Although I had belonged to the teen girls CGIT group at our previous church, this was one activity in my long list of things I was not going to do. Mom decided to lead Explorers, the younger girls group, as she had done in Port Coquitlam, and she asked me to help her. I had had a previous positive connection with Explorers in Port Alberni and had also enjoyed working with Mom in Brownies in Ladysmith, so I agreed. I was in charge of the stories, devotionals, and music, and she looked after everything else. This worked well for a few years. It was good to work with her, as we didn't spend that much time together otherwise.

Trinity Memorial United Church, Abbotsford

I had started to look for a new piano teacher when Dad came up with a plan. Finally, he saw the advantages of me playing the organ for him in church. He was convinced I could do this with a bit more training. Since he was going to continue paying for the lessons, he made the arrangements. This would prove disastrous. A very expensive teacher who came into Abbotsford from the United States each week to teach other organists agreed to take me on. Dad must have amplified my success for her to consider me. I would have lessons just on the organ. We'd alternate weeks

47

between my home organ and the big church organ. However, I found I could not possibly keep up with her expectations as I hadn't had sufficient grounding in the basics. It would have been better if I had made arrangements that I felt comfortable with. I was angry and frustrated with my father for not allowing me to start lessons when I had first asked as a child and for now placing me in this impossible situation.

One Sunday, Dad was suddenly stuck for an organist for his small subsidiary church and insisted I play. I could only play the hymns I already knew. I didn't want to do it, but he insisted. The first hymn was disastrous. I finished playing the fourth verse, but the people kept on singing…they were only on the second verse. Dad stopped us all, and we started over, slower. It was terribly embarrassing. On the way home, my father told me that it would be better the next time. I assured him there would not be a next time!

Soon after, Dad and I got into an argument over something not related to music. Again he prevailed. Well, not quite. I told him I was quitting music forever. That certainly punished him! But also me. This would be an extended and unfortunate break from church music that would have repercussions later in my life. The result was that I would never be able to offer leadership in church music without extreme difficulty.

However, I remember being part of choosing music with my parents. Once a week, when we had afternoon tea, we would choose the songs for the next service.

Mom would then phone the pianist with these selections. She had a chart that helped us to not repeat nor forget hymns. We started with one or two that closely worked in with Dad's sermon. I enjoyed being part of this. However, I did note that Dad never wanted a hymn that emphasized sin, the cross, or the shed blood of Jesus. Later, I would come to understand that salvation through Jesus was not a clear part of his belief system. I believed that Jesus' blood was shed for us so that we could have forgiveness of our sins. I felt, and feel now, that this is central to Christian faith. It wasn't surprising, then, that I slowly began to separate even more from my father's church.

Nearly every Saturday night the entire time I lived with my parents, I went to the church with Dad to get everything ready for the service the next day. One of my jobs was to put the hymn numbers on the board. Most people who have attended church in the past are familiar with the boards at the front of the church where number cards were arranged to show the hymns for that Sunday in order. There was a holder for all the spare numbers. I had started this fun job many years earlier, but Dad often had to make corrections. Soon he didn't need to bother, as I got them right most of the time. The times when I did make a mistake would just cause a ripple of laughter in the congregation as most people knew this was my job. Dad would make a good-natured comment.

I also tidied things up in the pews, on the back tables, etc. This included behind the pulpit. Those pulpits had a few shelves and held many things. If anyone needed a bandage, an aspirin, a tissue, a pin, a pencil, extra paper, a paper clip, and so on, that was a good place to look. However, it was also a convenient place to store unneeded "junk." Each week, I cleared out the unnecessary items and reorganized the rest. Also, I put a fresh but not full glass of water out of sight on the front right of the top shelf in case Dad had a coughing spell. To this day, I chuckle at the sight of ministers preaching at music stands or clear pulpits. Perhaps these new pulpits reflect the wish of ministers to eliminate barriers of any sort between themselves and their congregation. However, I cringe when people on the stage openly hold and use large travel mugs. Those old pulpits unobtrusively held many necessities for the minister and congregation. God's Word sustained the soul, but the pulpit contents assisted people in practical ways when unexpected emergencies came up.

There was a young couple in that church who would play an important part in my life. The man was on the church board. They had some very young children, and her children's needs prevented the woman from being as active in the church as she once had been and would become again later. She helped ease the tense situation in our home simply by befriending me. I always felt I could talk to her without fearing she would report everything to my parents. She would be a stabilizing influence on me while I lived in Abbotsford. In fact, we have an active and valued friendship to this day.

That first summer, she and her husband invited a small group of young people, male and female, to their house for an evening of "sloppy joes" and games. Many of these young people would become my good friends. They were part of the very active, large church youth group, which met every Sunday and had monthly socials. I soon joined that group and remained active in it.

My father asked me to do a simple job for him. The church had a bell tower but no longer any bells. However, mechanisms were put in place so that records playing bell music could be used. He asked me to run this record player. I didn't need to go to church, just play the bells before the services. I still don't know if Dad had things all planned. To get to the choir loft, the members had to go through this tiny room where I was playing records. There were two services. The first service had a junior girls' choir about my age. I met them as they went by, and soon I became part of that choir.

So, without pressure from my parents, I gradually became part of the life in that new church. Once again, the church was a secure influence within our family. This was fortunate, as I would find life in my new school stressful. It is very difficult for a teenager to

51

move schools in the late teens. I had gradually established a good social life in Port Coquitlam, and I missed that group very much. It took a very long time for me to develop any kind of comfortable social life in Abbotsford. The school was larger, and there were more activities, but somehow I had trouble fitting in. I still struggled to maintain good marks. I did make a few friends besides those in the youth group and choir. However, by the time I graduated, I was relieved that this period of my life was over.

A Difficult Year
Unfortunately, that school had a grade thirteen. This was offered as an equivalent to first year at the University of British Columbia (UBC). I would rather have gone to university, but grade thirteen was cheaper, and my parents insisted I take it. This meant another year at home, just when I was anxious to get away from that influence and control.

Throughout this time, I had a new boyfriend. His father was pastor of a Mennonite Brethren Church. He was a grade ahead of me, so when I went into grade thirteen, he went to UBC. He was the older brother of one of my girlfriends at school. Due to a stutter, he was extremely shy. However, he was highly intelligent and a wonderful friend. We felt we were lucky to have met, as preachers' kids have more problems socially. However, neither of us felt comfortable in the other's church. So, we started skipping church. He came to pick me up "for church," and both fathers assumed we were at the other church. In reality, we were at Cultus Lake or any place except church. It took a while for the fathers to figure this out. They were not pleased!

Finally, the fathers forced us to separate when he was to go to UBC and I began grade thirteen. His father refused to help finance his son unless we parted. We knew he was influenced by false stories my Dad had told him. I was so angry I hopped a bus and went to Vancouver to look for a job instead of starting school. I stayed with my aunt, who felt it better I stay with her than somewhere on the street. When I went to bed, I often heard bits of conversations my aunt was having with Dad. She tried her best to mediate between Dad and me, while also lovingly counseling me. Following three weeks of silence from me, the fathers reluctantly agreed to give my boyfriend and me some freedom to see each other when he was home. I returned to Abbotsford but was nearly not accepted back to the school due to my late enrolment. It was very hard to catch up. That crisis made living with my parents more difficult. It would take years to repair the damage done by their interference. Soon, I and this boyfriend would part anyhow. The main reason we stuck together as long as we did was to fight a common enemy.

Depression, Salvation, and Division

Also, during those years in Abbotsford, I had often become seriously depressed. My depression became so bad that I once again contemplated suicide. I felt ugly and alone and just could not carry the heavy burden around any longer. I developed a plan and waited for my parents to leave for the evening. I was in my upstairs bedroom, my head on my arms on my desk, crying. The window above the desk was open, and I faintly heard hymn music.

Just below our hill was a large Pentecostal church. I knew they were having a week of revival meetings with a visiting evangelist. My father had made many negative comments about this when we had been driving by. I remembered my interest in my Baptist friend's church several years earlier. I had always felt so good there. That night, I decided to postpone my plans. I ran down the hill and went into the church, even though I was a little late. I had left a note on the kitchen table saying where I had gone.

That night, I heard about salvation through Jesus Christ. I learned that if I accepted Him as my Savior, my many sins would be forgiven, and I would be assured of eternal life. Jesus would be my close Friend and walk with me and help me through my many personal problems in life. I had heard about this in the Baptist church but thought that only Baptists could have this salvation. Here I heard that anyone could be "born again," no matter what church they attended or even if they had never gone to church. I knew I needed forgiveness. I knew I needed Jesus as my Friend. In fact, I needed all the help Jesus could give me in life. I went forward when the altar call was given. A lady escorted me to a side room and explained salvation more completely to me. There I accepted Jesus Christ as my personal Savior. I was assured that He had forgiven all my sins through His blood shed on the cross. Finally I felt peace, as now I had a loving Companion who would be with me for the rest of my days and into eternity. Never again would I feel truly alone. I shed tears of joy.

When I told the lady who my father was, she went to get the evangelist and minister. They talked to me. I told them that I had been ready to end my life but now my father would likely do it for me! They assured me that if I went home and quietly explained what had happened, my parents might not be pleased, but they'd learn to adapt to it. This was especially true as I had years earlier voiced similar beliefs. They prayed for me and sent me home. They underestimated my father and the problems my decision would create.

Indeed, my parents were completely devastated by the time I came home. They had read my note and were sitting having tea, waiting for my return. I never did tell them that the evening had come close to being much worse. My father was so angry that he dragged me back to the church just as they were closing the building. They tried to calm him down, but everything they said made him angrier. He told us all that if I ever entered that church again, he'd call the police and have them arrested. They must have known this couldn't happen, but I certainly didn't.

The churches involved did not handle this delicate situation well. Some people in the Pentecostal church boasted about the minister's daughter who had been saved in their service. Several people in our church indicated displeasure that I'd put my father in such a position. They made me feel very ashamed and guilty. For some reason, even a few of my Mennonite Brethren friends at school were not pleased. I was very confused and conflicted.

My parents explained to me the charismatic nature of the Pentecostal church. I asked if I could go to a Baptist church, or maybe go to our church on Sunday mornings and then attend evening or weekday gatherings in another church. The answer was that I could go to no church except Dad's until after I left home.

Immaturely, in retaliation, I removed myself from most church connections for a time. This was unfortunate, as the church itself had done me no wrong. I had no interest in any church when I left for university. During the time I was at university, I rarely attended church except when home for a visit. This was not mature Christian behavior.

It was unfortunate that I did not have the opportunity to be helped and guided within an evangelical church. My life for many years reflected a lack of growth following my salvation. However, I was very fortunate that this event did happen. In future years, I would come to remember it well.

A Long and Difficult Engagement

The summer before I was to start university, I met a man quite a bit older than I was. His family had been deported from Hungary, but he had done well for himself working on the construction of pipelines in the north. He'd returned to his home in British Columbia's Lower Fraser Valley because he now had enough money to get married and support a family. He decided I was the one he'd marry.

In those days, one had to be age twenty-one to marry without parental consent. I had three years to wait. However, he showered me with love and gifts. My friends were impressed, as he had a nice car and a boat and he gave me many gifts. He was Lutheran but willing to attend my parents' church.

Soon, I was going to university wearing a huge engagement ring. For years, I had longed for the freedom to do as I wished. Now I was free of my parents, but I had a fiancé who came into Vancouver every weekend. Maybe this was good, as he somewhat curtailed any loose social life I might otherwise have become involved in. However, he was very controlling and manipulative. Many difficulties came up. After a two-year engagement, we postponed our planned summer wedding. When I was finished university, I returned home, and we tried to reconcile. I started working at a Bata shoe store for the summer and seeing him in the evenings. We tried to salvage our relationship, but it seemed to be getting worse. I was so upset and confused that health problems developed from the stress.

Once again, the United Church provided a safe haven for me. My dad inquired if there were any jobs available at Naramata Camp on Okanagan Lake. This was a camp that offered numerous programs for individuals and families. The United Church had adopted a new Sunday school curriculum. Many teachers were having trouble adapting to its changes. For a few years, Naramata hosted family camps where Sunday school teachers could come and bring their families. The instruction consisted of small teaching teams demonstrating how to conduct classes using the new curriculum. The families' children were the students. I had completed my teacher training and so was placed on one of these teams. There were three in our team, including one male. We became good friends as we worked together over the summer.

My accommodation was in an orchard cabin with several other girls my age or older and also a "house mother." There were several such small cabins, plus dorms attached to the main building. A separate building was used to prepare and serve meals. Many of the families who attended the camp stayed in the campgrounds.

Dad's idea turned out to be a good one although I had resisted it at first. Naramata provided me with a partial break from my fiancé for several months. However, he came up to Naramata many weekends, towing his boat. He seemed to be insanely jealous of any male companions included in our teams. While at Naramata, I was able to see more clearly the troubles we were having and accept that I could never fix them. I had people there to talk to. On one of those weekend visits, I returned his ring. Formerly, I had been unable to muster the courage to do this. However, the other camp leaders provided me with the support and encouragement I needed both before and after this final break.

Love and Marriage

In the fall, I returned to the Lower Fraser Valley for my first teaching job in Langley. I sometimes went to visit my parents on the weekend and attended church with them. One Sunday, there was a handsome new young man from Saskatchewan sitting alone. He worked for the Department of Transport at the airport. I sat with him, and we talked. His name was Barry Miller. My mother invited him for supper, and then he drove me home to Langley.

Very soon, we were engaged. He had just broken up with a girl. We both married on the "rebound," after knowing each other only five months. During some of those months, he was sent to the Queen Charlotte

Islands (now Haida Gwaii) and could only communicate by mail and an occasional phone call. However, we knew enough about each other to recognize we had met the type of person we could envision spending the rest of our lives with. We did love each other and felt this would grow. We have now been married over fifty-five years!

At the end of June, my parents moved to Sardis, B.C. We set the wedding date for July 1, 1966 in Sardis. Both the Abbotsford and Sardis churches were very supportive of this wedding, and we are still thankful for all their help. The Abbotsford ladies held a bridal shower for me; there was a wonderful turnout of loving ladies and many gifts. Maybe because there would be no big church wedding, many of the gifts were larger than typical shower gifts.

A kind lady in Abbotsford had a beautiful flower garden and made lovely flower bouquets for my one bridesmaid and me, plus the boutonnieres for the groom and best man. Another lady, from Sardis, filled that church with blooms for the wedding. The Abbotsford women sent sweets for the luncheon following the wedding, and the Sardis women provided the sandwiches and catering. We only had about twenty people in attendance. Barry's parents and his two younger sisters flew out for the wedding, and there were also some other relatives and friends.

I don't think Barry and I would have ever considered a wedding except at a church, performed by a minister. We even had our bans read in church for three weeks prior to the wedding. However, at one point, my father and I were arguing on the phone about something to do with the wedding. During the heat of this argument, Dad said that if I wouldn't agree to his wishes, he would not perform the wedding. I fired him, and we hung up! The alternative plan was to get married at the small United Church near where I had boarded during the past year and where I had attended on Sundays when not in Abbotsford. However, reconciliation happened, and plans proceeded for Sardis. No matter what or where, we would have insisted on a church and a minister for our wedding. It was important for us to have the blessing of the church upon our marriage.

Following a very short honeymoon, Barry resumed work at the Abbotsford Airport, and I took a job teaching in Mission, B.C. We attended the United Church in Abbotsford together. We even attended the couples' club. Every month, this group met at a home for a brief Bible study and visiting. There was also a social every other month. We were the youngest couple in attendance, but we were made to feel very welcome. It seemed strange to have a different minister in Dad's previous pulpit. However, the people in the church were pleased to have us. We certainly felt accepted and comfortable there.

Chapter 5
Early Marriage
Ladner and Abbotsford, B.C., 1966–1969

When Barry and I were first married, the church was central to our lives. However, life would take us in different directions quite quickly. The second year we were married, Barry was stationed at the Vancouver Airport. I managed to get a job teaching in Ladner, B.C. We lived there, and Barry commuted. Often he had night shifts. The third year, Barry was moved back to Abbotsford, and I worked only briefly as a substitute teacher. During those two years, our church attendance became more sporadic.

During the previous year, I had become pregnant, but that pregnancy had ended in miscarriage. Soon I was pregnant again. Between these two events, Barry purchased a farm. Life was changing drastically!

During our whirlwind courtship, Barry had mentioned that he'd like to possibly farm with his dad if land adjacent to his father's farm in Saskatchewan became available. It isn't possible to get started in farming unless relatives are willing to share machinery

63

with you to begin with. Suitable land didn't come available easily, so if Barry really intended to farm, he had to take the two quarters of land that were for sale then. It would be years before more suitable land was for sale; we were then able to purchase that as well.

My parents were not delighted with this decision. They had both been raised on the prairies and had often remarked how glad they were they had moved to temperate British Columbia. Most likely, I had not given the idea of farming enough thought and consideration before marriage. I had no idea what to expect, so I could not have had thoughts one way or the other. However, having our own house and not continually moving did appeal to me. Some of the homes in Saskatchewan did not have running water, but ours did. We would have a separate, private yard from Barry's parents and yet be close. It would turn out that I would experience extreme difficulties adapting to such a different lifestyle and type of family. Due to my youth, I went with a positive and optimistic attitude.

I would really miss my parents, and also my dad's sisters and their families in Vancouver. I had grown up with all those cousins. However, my mom's relatives lived quite close to us in Saskatchewan, and there were many cousins I could come to know. Although Barry's parents did not seem to love me, I was hopeful that if I proved I could be a good farmer's wife, they'd come to respect me. My parents would subsequently move closer in their two next pastoral positions and eventually retire in Yorkton, a small city close by.

Chapter 6
The Challenges
of Farm Life
Foam Lake, Saskatchewan, 1969–1988

The move to a Saskatchewan farm was a challenge. In future years, we would have huge gardens and an orchard. Later, I would raise poultry and learn to help with the farming. The big yard and surrounding bush would be a perfect place to raise a family. I planted my first garden that spring, but we didn't harvest much of it, as our daughter was born at the end of August.

A week after our daughter was born, I had a serious stroke. This was extremely unusual for a young person. Unknown to us, the fetus had a different blood type than I did, and this set up a condition that caused blood clots in me. Perhaps if we had remained in British Columbia for the entire pregnancy, this condition might have been recognized and treated and the problem prevented. The day I had the stroke, I was taken by ambulance to our local town hospital and was then quickly sent on to Saskatoon University Hospital.

Our baby was cared for in the local hospital until harvest was completed, and then Barry's parents and extended family looked after her.

When I came out of the coma a few days later, everything was difficult. My head hurt a great deal, and I could not swallow or move parts of my body for several days. When I became able to think, I grew concerned. Since the cause of the stroke had not yet been determined, I realized I could possibly have another one and not survive. When I requested that a chaplain visit, a United Church minister came. I explained that I wanted him to help me be ready to face death. I needed to be sure I was right with God and would go to heaven. Instead of being helpful, he chastised me for having such a negative attitude. He told me the doctors were trying their best and there had been some improvement, so I should just concentrate on achieving full recovery. My response was that I could more fully focus on this if I was not worried about my soul in the event of death. He became quite agitated and said he'd check in with me in a few days to see if I had become more positive. I told him to not bother. I should have requested an evangelical pastor.

My parents had flown immediately to Saskatoon to be with me. I remember being touched when I heard that my daughter's birth and my precarious health had been announced from the pulpits of most of the churches Dad had ministered in. I received notes from many of the people we had known. The love I had felt in the United churches in B.C. helped sustain us all. How fortunate I was to have had so many people praying for our family.

I did recover and a month later returned to our farm and daughter. Our life together in the farming community resumed. However, I had not achieved total recovery, as some of my short-term memory was missing. Unfortunately, this included parts of the four previous months when we'd first moved from B.C. During that time, I had been introduced to many family members and people in the community. However, now I didn't recall them all. When people greeted me, I often could not remember them or their names. I accidentally overheard a conversation about how badly I was doing. Thereafter, I became afraid to ask for names and so went years not fully remembering who some people were. This certainly put me at a disadvantage in my new life that many did not realize I was struggling with.

Church Struggles

Foam Lake (the closest town to our farm) had a United Church. The minister had been involved with the Miller family for many years and had helped them in previous times of difficulty and bereavement. Since my husband's parents and young sisters attended the United Church, it seemed best that I continue there. I really wanted and needed to fit into that church, and it started very well. The minister and his wife soon had me involved in helping them run a midweek children's ministry. I felt accepted and useful. It was a good start to prairie life.

However, some problems started quite quickly. I didn't believe in infant baptism. I felt this was a step people should take later when they were older and had accepted Jesus as their Savior. That first minister understood when we refused baptism for our daughter and did not allow others to pressure us. However, this set us apart within the church and disturbed our families.

The baptism issue became a greater problem in the years ahead when that minister moved away. The next minister was less understanding when we refused baptism for our adopted baby boy. More conflict over this issue would arise in years to come. The church later decided children could take communion if they had been baptized and understood what it was about. I felt some of our children were ready, but often the elements were not offered to them. Baptism became a painful issue. I wanted to fit in yet couldn't contradict my beliefs. Gradually, my husband had stopped attending church with me on a regular basis. I seriously reconsidered my own future in that church. However, I hesitated to change churches as I did not want to increase family conflict.

Later, three of our teen children, including a foster daughter, were confirmed one year, along with several others. However, our children needed to be baptized before they could be confirmed. I believe baptism is a public witness of belief, so I was happy this would happen. For confirmation, the minister made the sign of the cross on the forehead of each teen and said a blessing. He placed our three at the end nearest the baptismal font. For them, he simply dipped his finger in the water and said the same blessing. Nobody in the congregation, except our family, realized they were being "baptized." This wasn't much of a testimony! Later we'd learn that these "baptisms" weren't even recorded. Two of those teens would later be baptized again, in other congregations.

Foam Lake United Church

We had fostered one Cree handicapped girl and adopted one Assiniboine boy. Three other boys were also adopted. In today's culture, we'd say there was

71

"systemic racism" within the community. However, I certainly had not expected that within the church. Two of the boys were brothers of Dutch descent, aged four and five. Even they were not readily welcomed into the congregation. People are more accustomed to adoption of babies than youngsters. However, God's love should have enabled church people to overlook the boys' color or origins and show them total acceptance. It didn't help that one boy was poorly behaved and caused trouble in the Sunday school and church. No help was offered, just painful judgment. I know my father would not have allowed this within his church. He would have visited and talked to the family, to encourage, offer help, and come up with some solutions with us.

I can't entirely fault that church for my gradual and then final separation from it. I had my own serious problems. It was a great struggle for me to adapt to a farming lifestyle. It was difficult to have so few people to interact with daily. My husband's family was very different from my family in B.C., and family support was often lacking. I had never experienced such loneliness. Once again, I often struggled with severe depression, and my behavior often reflected this. Instead of help, I received criticism and neglect. I regret that because of these problems, I often was not fully engaged with the church or even with God. This caused some of our children to have difficulty finding the full spiritual stability and guidance they deserved as they grew up. I deeply regret not being a better Christian parent.

Just as I was again seriously considering leaving that church, our young teen daughter had become so advanced in music that she became the church organist. Within a year, she was also directing the choir. It was apparent that her future would be with music. Her job at the church, with all the resulting weddings and funerals, became a source of revenue for her. More importantly, it helped prepare her for the years ahead. She eventually became a symphony conductor. However, this necessitated me remaining in that church for many more years.

I tried very seriously to get involved in the church again. Initially, I had to drive our daughter to choir functions, so I joined the choir for a few years. I enjoyed the singing and interacting with the other choir members. However, when a throat condition made it impossible for me to continue singing, I just brought my daughter and sat in the back with our two small, recently adopted boys. It didn't feel as if anyone missed me at all or was interested in these changes.

Another minister couple soon came to the church. He and his wife were much more understanding of our complex family situation and my beliefs. However, the United Church as a whole was becoming more liberal. The time to leave had finally come, as my daughter was graduating from high school and leaving for university. The last Sunday she played, I remember sitting in church as others filed out. Her last note of the final postlude was my predetermined signal to end my relationship with the church I was raised in. I sat very still and prayed that God would bless my next fearful steps into unknown terrain.

A Desperate Time

That summer, our family encountered a series of crises. I became extremely ill due to a new aerial spray used for desiccating lentils. The planes took off from our neighbor's runway before heading to its next destination. Chemical was drifting everywhere. It was the first and last year that chemical was used. Many gardens were lost because of it, and several frail people died. I was nearly one of them. Gradually, I became unable to retain food or fluids and could only consume a few small cups of warm honey water and half a peach a day. Eventually, I was unable to manage even this meager diet and nearly died from dehydration and weight loss.

Nevertheless, I continued preparing food for our large family. While the others were eating, I would go outside and lie on the grass under the apple tree. When they had finished eating, I would return, do the dishes by myself, and go to bed. This was the busy harvest season when the family had less time and energy to recognize my rapid decline or my need for help. Normally, I had been requiring the children to help me with the chores, but by this time there was no energy to call for help. Maybe they were just happy not to have their usual chores and did not want to ruin their good fortune by asking questions.

This might seem surprising, but chaos always reigned during harvest season, and life was never normal. I felt invisible to my family. Eventually, living felt unbearable, and I became desperate. One night, I totally came to the end of my ability to cope. Once again, I came very close to suicide. I made plans to leave the next day. But God intervened to stop my plans in several ways that could only be considered miraculous.

Barry had been struggling with a sore back for several days. That evening, he was suddenly thrown to the floor in unbelievable pain, and I had to stay to help him. I located the local doctor at the bowling alley and tried to convince him to come to the farm and give Barry an injection. He told me he never visited farm homes. I told him I was on the way into town to pick him up. He came, gave the injection, left additional pills, and told me to get Barry to the hospital in Regina the next morning. He said that he would contact the hospital and felt that Barry would need back surgery. Somehow, God had given me the ability to convince that doctor to do what he had never done previously — or since.

Barry had been to see a chiropractor earlier that week; as he drifted off to sleep, he told me to contact that man in the morning. He wondered if he could help us avoid going to Regina. I phoned him the next morning, but it was Sunday, and he had just left for church. His wife explained that following church he was going somewhere else and would not be home until evening. I left a message with her. However, it turned out that he had left something behind and returned home before going to church. He got my message, remembered Barry, and phoned us. We were told to meet him at his office. That hour-long drive was difficult for us both, but the chiropractor helped Barry. He also noticed how poorly I was doing and gave me some help. We would both need more medical help, but we left his office somewhat improved. We came to recognize that God had caused him to return home, get our message, and agree to help us on the Sabbath.

When we got home, we found our combine was sitting in the field, full of grain and waiting for a truck to unload into. Our family communication was so poor that Barry's father had not realized that he had nobody to truck the harvested grain. Barry was still in too much pain, and I was too weak. I convinced our sixteen-year-old son to drive the truck. He had just received his driving license but had no experience with trucking. I went along as a passenger and told him what to do. This was a very difficult field to truck from. It was right beside the Yellowhead Highway, and there was extra traffic on the long weekend. Each load had to cross that busy road, starting from an uphill stop. It could have been disastrous if the truck had stalled trying to cross the highway. Somehow we got through that day without an accident.

During the day, Barry's mom had sent out a snack of cheese buns. They looked good, but I hadn't been able to eat for weeks. There were no bathroom facilities if I had a problem, and I was with my son and in clear view of the busy highway. However. I managed to eat half a bun. It stayed with me. She later sent supper to our home. I ate a bit and even had some water. All seemed well. I knew for sure God was working!

When everyone had gone to bed, I sat in the living room and thought about all that had happened. God had powerfully intervened in so many ways. Only He could have done all that! I knew then that He did not want me to die. Even though I had felt invisible to my family, He had seen and cared. This all caused me to remember how I had accepted Jesus as my Savior those many years ago in the Pentecostal church in Abbotsford. I reflected that I had not walked closely with Him for many years. Weeping with remorse, I repented of my sins and rededicated my life to Jesus. If possible, I wanted to live, truly live—physically, emotionally, and spiritually. My sins and years of spiritual neglect were forgiven. God did not instantly cure me, but He was with me through a long and difficult recovery.

It would take three years for me to gradually return to health and regain my normal weight. Chemical sensitivities became a long-lasting result. For the next five years, I was extremely allergic to perfumes, hair sprays, laundry products, etc. Many foods remained a problem for the rest of my life. That was an extremely challenging time to enter a new church. However, I knew I needed a spiritual connection badly, no matter how difficult it would be. I had already planned on changing churches that fall. Now, having rededicated my life to Jesus, I was more convinced than ever that I had to go. I needed and wanted help and guidance from an evangelical church.

Taking Leave

I felt it was important for me to talk to the United Church minister and his wife. We had become friends over the years, sharing meals and working together. They had been good to us. I went to their house one evening, and we talked for hours. I told them that the other church wouldn't be "stealing sheep" because I had already decided to leave the United Church and the Gospel Fellowship Church was the only alternative that might be suitable. I also explained more fully my faith journey. They were sad, but we parted with hugs and good wishes. Our friendship would continue.

This decision was for me and the four children remaining in our home. My husband was left to decide his own church future. Perhaps that was not totally fair to him, but his absence from church made me feel I had this right. I am very grateful he was gracious about the change. God was already working on him.

My father, by this time, had retired and was living in a small city nearby. The Foam Lake United Church minister would soon develop cancer and need extended relief. It would fall upon my father to come and substitute. This became awkward, but this complication had not been foreseen when we left the United Church. By the time Dad came to preach, we were already involved in our new church, as the people there had quickly put us to work. However, whenever possible, one member of our family would go to be in Dad's congregation.

The United Church had been the foundation of my life and an anchor for my soul for many years. Within it, I had heard Bible stories and learned much about God. Many people in that denomination had played a vital role in developing my personality and my beliefs. I will forever cherish their many acts and words of kindness. Looking back, I realize it was an advantage being raised in the home of a United Church minister. Even on the prairies, the United Church often helped our family, especially our daughter and her music. I have much gratitude for what the United Church gave my family over the forty years I was part of it.

It was comforting to know that Granddaddy Moses had had beliefs similar to mine. When it had been formed in 1925, he had entered the United Church in the hope that this new denomination would retain at least some of his evangelistic zeal and Methodist beliefs. Combining the Methodist, Congregational, and

Presbyterian churches was a great advantage to tiny, struggling churches on the prairies. The founding ministers worked hard to find common ground on matters such as baptism. They had to make compromises in order to create larger churches that could have a more positive impact on their communities. However, Granddaddy would not have been pleased with some of the theological changes that later came into this church. I believe Moses would have approved of my beliefs. I really felt that Granddaddy's granddaughter was returning to the faith of her ancestors.

Chapter 7
The Mennonite Brethren Church
Foam Lake, Saskatchewan, 1987–2008

Before I write about our move to the Mennonite Brethren church, I should explain that it had already been a sustaining presence in the life of our family. Foam Lake had many people closely associated with the Ukrainian and Icelandic cultures, and many of the churches within that community reflected this. The Mennonite Brethren church was the only other Protestant church, except for a tiny Anglican one. Initially, I would have assumed the Mennonite Brethren church was purely for members of the Mennonite cultural group.

Two of our neighbors were Mennonite Brethren. The couple closest to us lived a fifteen-minute walk away. The wife often invited me for tea. Even after we had a family, I'd walk down, pushing a baby stroller or pulling a sled. She had a huge garden in front of her house that I walked by to get to her door. I had no idea how to plant a garden or how to process what grew. The very slow walk by her garden was so educational. Often she'd ask if I'd like to go back out and walk in her garden. I sure did! She seemed to know that I needed help but was too proud to ask. She taught me a great deal, yet never made me feel inferior. We also shared sewing and other projects as the years went on.

When I sat at this couple's table having tea, our talk often turned to religion. They had a mini bookcase on their table holding books about faith, and I often borrowed some. At times, I challenged their faith using my dad's perspective. They didn't know I was testing them. I always felt good that they were able to disagree with my stated challenges in ways that actually supported my own beliefs. However, I wasn't ready to join them. There was the matter of how I could change my biological roots to become Mennonite. I did not yet understand that their faith and their culture were two separate entities.

This woman's sister-in-law lived on the other side of our farm. That lady's third child was a boy the same age as our first adopted boy. Our relationship developed as we cooperated over many years in transporting children to and from skating and swimming lessons and other activities. Also, for many years, she picked up our children every Wednesday evening for "club," which was an interdenominational children's group meeting in their church. Every summer, they hosted a morning "Vacation Children's

Camp" for a week in August. Again, she picked up our children so they could attend. At the end of the week, the children put on a program, and the parents were invited.

Four or five churches from surrounding towns, including the one in Foam Lake, had a church camp at Fishing Lake close to our home. All of our children went to at least a few of these camps. Our children also attended the Mennonite Brethren youth group, as the United Church didn't have one. These kind neighbors and the many programs at their church gave me an opportunity to observe them in action. These activities greatly supplemented the Sunday school of the United Church. I am so grateful for that extra spiritual help and guidance for our children.

During my first years in Saskatchewan, the local Mennonite Brethren church changed its name to Foam Lake Gospel Fellowship Church. This was an effort to make non-Mennonites feel welcome. I was still not convinced I could truly belong. Then, for a short time, there was a "split" in the church. By this time, our oldest children were in the church's youth group. Those young people stayed together, no matter what was going on with the parents. The split was soon resolved, and the two sides began worshiping together again. Strangely, when I saw that they weren't perfect, I thought maybe I would fit there after all.

In the meantime, two younger pastors had come and gone from that church. The next pastor and his wife came from British Columbia. They were older, and their children were grown. This would be their last pastorate. They built a house and were looking for a rug about the time I was selling mine. Chemical allergies had caused me to react to the smell of this newer rug. I remember our short visit. I knew I was coming closer to the time when we would finally be ready to come to the Mennonite Brethren church. I didn't quite get up the nerve to invite them for tea. I really needed to talk to them, but I hesitated. Soon, I would be even more ready to talk to them. When I was, they would be waiting and welcoming.

Taking the First Steps

Near the end of the summer of 1987, I took the four boys who were still living at home to the Gospel Fellowship Church. It was difficult yet exciting for us all. When the people understood the nature of my chemical illness, the entire church made efforts to use fewer perfumes and similar products. The boys quickly became part of the Sunday school. The older two boys continued their participation in the youth group. One joined a small church band that performed about once a month. That ensemble gave a reason for Barry to start coming on occasion. Soon, he was there more often. They quickly gave him the job of running the sound system, so he felt needed.

My husband didn't personally find my move difficult initially. His family was unhappy about this change when they heard about it. However, there was nothing they could say, as my husband hadn't been going to church with me for years. My parents struggled with it but couldn't have been surprised. They felt insecure about how to continue their involvement with the United Church in Foam Lake. However, that was somewhat resolved as they saw my continuing good relationship with the sick minister and his wife.

Original Gospel Fellowship Church

Although I shared the essential salvation beliefs with my new church, I quickly realized how much I didn't know about the Bible and theology. I started attending Wednesday evening Bible studies. Being somewhat bold in nature, I quite freely asked questions there, as well as at adult Sunday school. I was surprised during the resulting discussions that many of the attenders disagreed with each other on various topics. The pastor, however, seemed to relish this "shake up" and never discouraged any questions. Finally, people were not trying to keep me quiet! I was heard and helped.

After Christmas, the church started Sunday evening classes and invited the entire congregation. I would later understand that they were using "baptismal class" materials. Usually only people interested in adult baptism attended these yearly classes. However, the many previous discussions had caused the church board to think it would be good for everyone to attend as a "review." I loved that time! Following the final class, I asked the pastor if I could be baptized that summer. In the end, I was one of eight people who were baptized. My oldest son joined me. It was a very special time indeed.

The church didn't have a baptismal tank, so waited until summer and used the local lake at the church camp. Later groups would make use of the new swimming pool in town. The day started with a church service where each of the candidates gave a testimony.

That afternoon, we gathered at the lake for the baptisms and then returned to the church for communion.

In my testimony, I said that I still valued knowing that my granddaddy Moses had baptized me as a child. I felt that through adult baptism I was confirming the faith he would have wanted for his first granddaughter. I felt very close to him that day.

This was a bit of a confusing time for my husband. Some in the church had suggested I wait until my husband wanted to join me. My answer was that I was ready. I didn't want Barry to feel pressured into it. However, the church was sensitive to his feelings and wanted to be sure he was comfortable with me doing this. The pastor talked to him and received his blessing. His parents did not attend. My parents just attended the baptism at the lake. The only sad part of that day for me was my mother crying as she stood watching. I remember making eye contact with my husband just before I was submerged. The Lord revealed to my heart that he would soon do what I was doing. Indeed, within a few years, he and two more sons were baptized, and Barry and I have shared a common faith ever since. I am very thankful. God is so good!

Growing Deeper

Barry and I had many challenges raising a family. Soon, some terrible and unexpected problems came upon us. The pastor couple and the entire church greatly helped our family. We felt encouraged, loved, and strengthened. That church was by no means perfect, but it helped us through many difficult times. All of our boys felt very accepted. Three of them had learning or behavior problems, but the church seemed happy to work with these difficulties. Our new church didn't gossip or judge us. They talked to us and to the boys, and together we came up with ways to deal with problems as they came up.

My husband Barry is a shy, quiet man. However, he was encouraged there and became a valuable asset to that church. Soon, a larger church was needed. A commercial building was purchased which would need an addition and drastic alterations. Barry became head of the building committee and worked on that over a few years until it was completed. Many changes were made after the move. He remained head of church maintenance until we retired to British Columbia. He also became the church treasurer. It was so good to finally go to church and be involved in its activities with my husband.

The first job I was elected to was to be a correspondent for the *Mennonite Brethren Herald*. This was a bi-monthly magazine sent to all of the denomination's church members in Canada. My job was to send information about baby dedications, baptisms, weddings, and deaths. However, I could also contribute stories and articles. I sent several over the years, and some were printed. The editors also asked me to write book reviews, mostly for new children's books. My children enjoyed those books with me.

Present Gospel Fellowship Church

Over the next twenty years, I became even more involved in church activities. Within a few years, I was elected Sunday school superintendent. I kept this job for eighteen years until we moved to British Columbia. The Mennonite Brethren church recognized my training and abilities and put them to good use. This gave me joy and a renewed purpose in life. It helped me regain self-confidence and my sense of worth. I was useful and valued once again. I still had problems, both personally and within the church, but I was never judged. We all tried to help each other overcome obstacles in life.

That church had Sunday school for everyone from 10:00 to 10:50 a.m., and the church service started at 11. The adult class was quite large. I was responsible for selecting materials for all ages as well as getting teachers. Eventually, the teaching in the adult class was shared by several teachers, including myself. I also substituted as a teacher for the children's classes as needed.

Every year, I wrote and directed a Sunday school Christmas concert and an Easter program. The creative process was fun and good for me. My valued assistant provided great help and fellowship. I felt it was important for children to be able to participate in these dramas at their own personal comfort level. I tried to make sure every child, over a period of a few years, had opportunity to be a wise man, a shepherd, or an angel or some other character in costume. Also, I felt it was memorable for each child to light a candle.

The Ladies' Aid group sewed many costumes. Barry built a wardrobe cupboard on wheels to store these. It was wonderful to work on joint projects with him. We participated in so many more activities in that fellowship. The church became our lifeblood. We felt renewed throughout those busy years.

I was also involved in arranging children's features in the church service twice a month. Five of us usually took turns doing this. I organized a Christian Education Sunday once a year. The Sunday school supported and corresponded with a missionary. Every year, there was a church picnic in June to organize. This all kept me very busy in a variety of ways.

Even my childhood wish to be church pianist was partly fulfilled. I had started practicing playing hymns again. Often we would sing one hymn at the start of the Wednesday evening prayer meeting, and I would play. That was a good beginning. When the pianist had to be away, I often substituted for the church service as well. I found this stressful with my limited ability, but I managed to get through the services. When our daughter came home for a visit, she would attend with us, and nearly always she would be asked to play the second keyboard to back up the pianist. She felt welcome there.

Meanwhile, I was taking correspondence courses from Briercrest College in Caronport, Saskatchewan. Over ten years, I earned a degree in Biblical Studies. A new, younger pastor came who was open to women in leadership. He asked me to lead Bible studies and sometimes Wednesday evening prayer meetings.

There was a period of time when our church had no minister. We hired guest speakers for Sunday mornings. However, many of us were called upon to take on other tasks. One of my extra jobs was running the care home service once a month. I played the piano and did the devotional, usually taking a small group with me. This small extra commitment influenced much of what I would do during retirement in the near future.

We remember those precious twenty years and all that we experienced within that church with great joy, love, and thankfulness. Problems were managed well by the pastors. The people encouraged each other when problems arose. Everyone seemed to watch for discouragement in each other and offered love, concern, and help when possible. We were made to feel precious and valued. Almost from the first days we attended that church, our talents and abilities were recognized, and we were given responsibilities that suited us. We were made to feel needed and accepted. Certainly, we never regretted our decision to be baptized again and become members. There our spiritual foundations were secured, and they became stronger throughout the years ahead.

Chapter 8
A Pause for Reflection
Elgin, Manitoba, 2008

We decided to sell the farm and retire in British Columbia. Barry's parents and then mine had passed away. Our boys were not interested in farming. We wanted to return to the area where I had grown up and where we had first met. We had a son and daughter in the Lower Fraser Valley in B.C.

However, before we left, we made a quick trip to visit our sons then living in Manitoba. I had been deeded some old family Bibles that had belonged to Granddaddy Moses Nixon. Inside one of them, I found two pictures. One was from a church in Saskatchewan where he had ministered before he was married. I tried but wasn't able to make many connections there.

However, the next picture was from Elgin, Manitoba. It showed a huge house with a carriage and horse in front. My father would likely have been a baby inside the carriage. I was able to make connections with that church, and it happened that they were going to be celebrating an anniversary year. We attended that event. When we walked in, we saw pictures of the various ministers who had served in that church. The first one was of Granddaddy Moses. I felt as if I had come "home."

I did a children's feature showing a photo of that house, a photo of my grandpa, and another photo of him and me. The main part of the feature was the actual Bible Grandpa had used in that church. I also had a brief part in the service, standing at the same pulpit Grandpa had used many years earlier. This was a great experience for me. My presence also seemed to be of great interest to many of the older people in the church.

Over the years when we were camping, we had often stopped at Rossburn, Manitoba. Grandpa Moses had at one time been a minister in the church there. Later, he retired to Rossburn. When he died, he was buried in a beautiful cemetery on a hill overlooking a vast valley. Grandma had then come to British Columbia and lived in an apartment near her daughters in Vancouver. Eventually, she lived with one of those daughters. When she died, her body was shipped to Rossburn to be buried beside Grandpa. We have taken our children there frequently. I always felt comforted when visiting Granddaddy's and Grandma's grave site.

Chapter 9
A Meaningful Retirement
Surrey, British Columbia, 2008–

We retired to, Chelsea Gardens, a gated community in Surrey, B.C. We had expected to experience a challenging readjustment. British Columbia's Lower Fraser Valley was so different from the place we had left forty years earlier. Our particular townhouse was on the end of a row of units. We had the only large green area in the complex. The foliage there was backed by the trees of a park across the street. We were happy for this spaciousness. It was hard to get used to traffic, with so many stores and large malls, but it was fun. At last, we were living among lots of people. The complex had a very active social life. so I never felt alone again.

We didn't expect to have difficulty finding a church to suit us, as there were many to choose from. We felt any evangelical church somewhat close in theology to the church we had left would be good. We wanted one close by so we wouldn't have to travel far. However, it was much harder than we expected to find a church that suited us. One thing we quickly found was that we just did not feel comfortable in the many large churches in the area. The average church attendance at our Mennonite Brethren church in Saskatchewan had been about fifty. We felt lost in the numerous large gatherings in the city.

In the fourteen years we have been in British Columbia, we have attended many churches. A few we attended for only a few short visits. Others we attended for longer periods of time. One thing that caused us to leave three churches was "church splits." We just didn't understand enough of what was going on. In a small rural church, when there were arguments or disagreements, solutions had to be found quickly. It wasn't possible to try another church without driving to another town. Also, in Surrey we had a few experiences of a minister resigning in the pulpit, effective nearly immediately, with no explanation. Now we're settled into a reasonably small Baptist church which we hope will be good for us as the years go on.

In our time back in British Columbia, we have found that we do not often hear a direct evangelical appeal. The invitation seems somewhat obscured. I know altar calls are a thing of the past, as are revival meetings. However, we feel the salvation message here often lacks the clarity we had grown accustomed to.

It could be assumed that I would seek to continue my involvement in Christian education in British Columbia. However, that has not happened at all. I discovered that Sunday school teachers usually have to miss church because there is not a separate Sunday school hour. Churches try to remedy this by having several teachers share each class or by amalgamating classes. The teacher's preparation for teaching and therefore the teacher's influence on the child becomes minimal. Christmas and Easter programs by the young people rarely happen. I am very concerned about the lack of spiritual education our young people are receiving. Certainly, my own childhood was much richer spiritually. It appears to me that the lack of emphasis on Christian education has had a hugely negative impact on our society.

An Unexpected Ministry

Our work has come to be with seniors. In Saskatchewan, we lost our four parents and my husband's younger sister all in four years. We helped each parent go through the painful process of trying to manage at home, then in care homes, and finally in hospitals. Along the way, I developed a deep passion for the many seniors around us, many of whom seemed alone. I would have thought that after our last parent died, I would never want to enter a seniors' facility again. However, after a short time, I found I did want to go back. In British Columbia, a seniors' ministry seemed to open up in our very first year.

First, we started an interdenominational Bible study within Chelsea Gardens. We managed to get permission to gather in the library of the clubhouse. For several years, our group presented a "Christmas Prelude" program during Advent and invited everyone within the complex. The first year, only forty-five attended. By the sixth year, we had one hundred and ten. The program room and overflow were completely filled. The event became too big for the space, and so we decided to end this practice the seventh year. Perhaps we will stage a similar program in the future, but we would not include such an extravagant lunch as we had been preparing. However, we found that the attitude of the people in Chelsea Gardens in general had become "softer" towards our group partly because of these programs.

Meanwhile, some of us started going to a care home to put on a service. There were some excellent singers in our Bible study group. I played the piano and provided the devotional. Soon, we had better musicians join the group, and I just worked on the program. We called ourselves the "Chelsea Messengers."

After a while, we accepted an invitation from a second care home. A third home invited us, but we felt going to a care home two Sundays a month was all we could handle. Others from Chelsea Gardens have joined us, so the team is no longer composed of just people from the Bible study. The members of the Bible study and the Chelsea Messengers are from different denominations, and it is wonderful working together.

Sometimes I would hear people complain about the modern music in their church or the lack of hymns. I would invite them to join us, as we sang seven to eight hymns each Sunday. I found putting together a program and devotional suitable for seniors was fun and challenging. I assigned others who were willing the chance to handle some parts of the program, such as Scripture readings. We present a varied and interesting program. This has been good for me, as well as uplifting for the seniors.

For about six years, I became a paid chaplain in two care homes. There, I offered a hymn sing program and used some of my devotional materials between the songs. I also enjoyed going into the rooms and visiting seniors personally. I well understood their difficulties, as we'd experienced similar issues with our parents not long before. Sometimes I was able to help with practical suggestions. Sometimes I prayed with them. Sometimes I just listened. I didn't enjoy the political tensions that arose within the care home staff, which I often seemed to somehow get dragged into. At age seventy-five, I officially retired from this short career.

Pandemic Pivots

During the COVID-19 pandemic in 2020 and 2021, I was impressed with the amount of effort our minister made to keep us all connected. We were able to watch online church on our TV from the comfort of our recliners. Although the Chelsea Gardens Bible studies were canceled, a group of us delved into Revelation as we met weekly online. That was a great time to study that challenging book. We all felt excited and reassured to know that God is in control of what is happening in our world today and in the future.

I also joined a ladies' online Bible study through our church. Previously, I hadn't had time for such a study. That was a great experience. I had previously been concerned that the call to salvation in the church was somewhat muted. However, I learned that each of the other eight ladies had personally accepted Jesus as their Savior. This reassured me that the gospel was being heard.

As I write this book, we are trying to emerge from the COVID-19 restrictions, but much confusion and uncertainty remain. Many did not get their vaccinations when they were available, and many have contracted a COVID variant. As we contemplate our future life, we are taking time to re-evaluate what activities to continue, change, or drop. We are confident God will direct us.

We ourselves are facing future years of uncertainty as we become older. So far, we have been able to be independent and help others who are struggling. However, we know our own problems will increase. We are grateful that we still have each other, yet we cannot assume that even this will continue. It is good to have a faith in God, who will uphold us no matter what our future holds. Our faith was developed from childhood on within various church denominations. We are both very grateful to all the churches that have been part of our lives.

Epilogue
My Life in Churches

I was fortunate to be a minister's daughter, as the church was an automatic extension of my family. I saw my parents work through struggles and triumphs as they interacted with many kinds of people. I learned to receive and offer encouragement, friendship, and help. I learned from my family's many moves that when you close the door to one phase of life, new doors will open ahead.

Above all, I am thankful that I heard the stories of Jesus as a young child. Eventually, I developed my own deep, personal faith in Jesus Christ as my Lord and Savior. I am so grateful to both the United Church and the Mennonite Brethren Church for their powerful influence in my life. Without their influence, I would have floundered and failed amidst the difficulties of life.

I encourage young people to base their marriage and family on the secure foundation of Christian faith. That can be most fully developed within the church. People in the congregation will positively augment the parents' influence on their children. Churches are not perfect. However, it is even educational for our young people to see Christian people wrestle with problems together. In time, churches resolve many human errors.

Today there are so many competing activities in society that it is harder for families to make the church their focal point. Many parents try to fit in church activities only as a secondary consideration. Also, churches are often not sufficiently capitalizing on the children who do or could be encouraged to come. Churches and families need to work together.

The present culture in society is increasingly ungodly, marked by media fixation, hate crimes, addictions, mental stress, depression, and even suicides. All these reflect the shifting sands that our children's lives are being built on. A stronger commitment to God would give families guidance as they face these problems together. God is unchanging and forever loving. He will strengthen and empower us if we place our faith in Him alone. Society needs more people and families seeking Him. A strong connection to the church is essential in maintaining and strengthening a personal connection with God.